My Favorite Quotes Collection

Volume III

My Favorite Quotes Collection

Volume III

By

Derrick D. Richardson

My Favorite Quotes Collection
Volume III

iUniverse books may be ordered through booksellers or by contacting:

iUniverse
1663 Liberty Drive
Bloomington, IN 47403
www.iuniverse.com
844-349-9409

ISBN: 978-1-4502-2374-4 (sc)
ISBN: 978-1-4502-2375-1 (e)

Print information available on the last page.

iUniverse rev. date: 08/17/2020

Also by Derrick D. Richardson

I Always Wanted To Do This

My Favorite Quotes Collection, Volume II

Once you qualify, people can justify.

Once you show someone you are worthy of their support, they can justify recommending you on a personal or professional level without being embarrassed or regretting making an introduction to someone in their circle of influence.

To my wonderful wife, Kathleen

To my family

Very special thanks for her powerful words of wisdom to

Sheila Goins

Contents

Preface

Dear Subscribers, Friends, Family, and Supporters:

Allow me to salute a hardy "thank you" for all of the endless support and belief you all have shown for my previous publications. This journey has been challenging, yet very rewarding for me. Without you all, my efforts to write would have not been as worthwhile.

Nevertheless, here I am again encouraged to complete my final publication. This third book will conclude my series of "books of quotations." With this said, I invite you to ride this journey with me through to the end. So, sit back, relax, and enjoy the conclusion of this matter.

In addition, as I hope you have come to realize, I, too, allow myself to relax while allowing my thoughts, my knowledge, my wisdom, and my experiences to guide me to precise quotations of real-life scenarios, real-life people, and real-life places.

In my previous publications, I purposely structured my books to allow my supporters the space to take notes directly on the pages, which was my wife Kathleen's idea. This third addition also encourages the subscribers to jot down their thoughts as they indulge in the contents of this final edition. So, as I share my final thoughts and quotes, I ask that you open your heart, your mind, and your imagination.

Although this is my final publication, I will forever be grateful to each of you.

Again, thank you,

Derrick Richardson, Author

Acknowledgments

I like to thank God.

As a human being, I forget about God sometimes.

I forget that all things go through him.

I forget that he doesn't put more on my plate than I can handle.

I forget that I am here to serve his purpose.

I forget that I am who I am because of him.

I have to remind myself every day that God is the reason I wake in the morning.

Introduction

<u>Stay in the Race</u>

You know, life seems to unfold in the most bizarre and challenging ways. It's as if life positions itself on the starting blocks, the gun goes off, and the life race begins. And, although running any race can pose various challenges, life's race feels quite rewarding, especially when all things pertaining to life seem to be "in the lead."

Yes, just like a runner out of the blocks who has pulled out front, way out front and is headed toward the finish line—yet, with still some distance ahead, the runner begins to smell the sweet aroma of victory. But then—it happens—another runner has gained the lead.

Not only did this other runner gain the lead, but this runner kicked dust and rocks in the face of the original lead runner! *Wow*! Isn't this the way life happens sometimes?

Just as we start running this life race, living the American dream, our situations and circumstances start gaining on us. Not only do they gain on us, but, because we took these situations and circumstances for granted, the dust and the rocks of these issues begin to impact the quality of the run, affecting our ability to complete the race—the life race.

Hmm. Then, just when the original lead runner—you, me, us—begin to dust off our faces, get the rocks out of our eyes, and gain a little confidence that everything is going be all right, we say to ourselves, "All we have to do is stay focused and the lead can be ours again." We say to ourselves, "The other runner can't be *that* far ahead." Then it happens—the runner, the other runner—*lapped* the original runner! My oh my! Could things get any worse for a runner who starting out this race *in the lead?*

Such is life. When we started this race, the crowd was cheering, "*Go, go, go,* you can do it, you can do it! Chase your dreams, go get what you want from this life." But that same crowd that was cheering you when you were in the lead now is *booing* you, telling you to *quit!* Especially since life's issues, situations, and circumstances now seemed to have *lapped* you.

So what do you do when you find yourself in this very spot? This very race! Hmm, well, I hope you will find that the answer to this scenario may seem difficult to embrace, especially under such circumstances. However, the answer can be simply found in the title of this little short story: Stay in the Race.

Allow the motivation of those who are trying to get you to quit to fuel your ability to stay in the race. Then, before long, that same crowd that tried to get you to quit will begin to cheer you on again. Why? Because they cannot believe that, against all odds, all trials, all elements, you *did not quit,* but you stayed in the race.

So, when you feel that you have been *lapped* in life, allow yourself to be encouraged by the message that it doesn't matter that life's issues may have lapped on you. What does matter is that you finish the race, my friends. Stay in the race.

Sheila Goins

In life, we must discover *courage, character, respect, dignity, honor,* and the *truth* in ourselves.

—Derrick D. Richardson

To be able to speak negatively about something, it has to have a history first.

—Derrick D. Richardson

If you can't reach the sky the first time you jump, grab onto something and gradually climb your way to the top.

—Derrick D. Richardson

Everyone wants to shine for someone. It's who you want to shine for that determines your character.

—Derrick D. Richardson

Money puts you in a circle that broadens your horizons and leads to exposure.

—Derrick D. Richardson

Life is given. Living is work.

—Derrick D. Richardson

If you protect your heart too long from love, it won't be any good when you decide to use it.

—Derrick D. Richardson

It takes more than your paycheck to provide a nice household. It also takes giving of yourself.

—Derrick D. Richardson

If you make it a habit of letting people know you know something, they're not going to want to hear from you anyway.

—Derrick D. Richardson

Doing your homework is the best training you can get.

—Derrick D. Richardson

Decisions of love are best made when at rest.

—Derrick D. Richardson

Money management is not always about saving money; it's also about spending it the right way.

—Derrick D. Richardson

If you keep looking behind you, you'll miss what's in front of you.

—Derrick D. Richardson

Battles are won on the battlefield. Wars are won in the office.

—Derrick D. Richardson

Real news isn't in the media, only enough news to satisfy the people—and even that news is old news.

—Derrick D. Richardson

It's not about the place to be or what if has to offer if a couple isn't connecting with each other, but when two people *are* connecting it doesn't matter where they are, as long as they are together.

—Derrick D. Richardson

When two people step out on a ledge together, the bond between them builds ground underneath their feet, and they never have to worry about falling off.

—Derrick D. Richardson

Being in love has its phases. What phase are you in?

—Derrick D. Richardson

You think about a lot of should've, would've, and could've sitting in hell.

—Derrick D. Richardson

The idea of going through something bad only to come out on the other end stronger is overwhelming because while you are going through it, you just want back what you had.

—Derrick D. Richardson

If people can see everything you own because you are wearing it or driving it, you don't have much.

—Derrick D. Richardson

Most young people don't realize they are in the best position to take risks. For most of us, the next time we are in a position to take risk again, we already have a lot on our plate.

—Derrick D. Richardson

Everyone is different depending on who they are around, but in our own comfort zone, we are not much different from each other.

—Derrick D. Richardson

Attaching yourself to a core vision is like the table salt in a salt shaker that sticks to the bottom. No matter how much you shake off the top, some still sticks.

—Derrick D. Richardson

When it comes to bringing home good grades, A's—not the D's—
is the goal. When it comes to bringing home girls, the opposite
is the goal.

—Derrick D. Richardson

People always say that you will know when you are ready to get married. But, until that time reaches you, you won't know it. The funny thing is, until you are ready to get married, you don't understand what they mean.

—Derrick D. Richardson

Facts are in black and white, not to be used to judge based on whether someone is black or white.

—Derrick D. Richardson

They say death and taxes are the two things certain in life. I say *change* is also certain in life.

—Derrick D. Richardson

You can't judge another man's character based on what you would do.

—Derrick D. Richardson

Even the smallest circle seems big if you don't travel it often.

—Derrick D. Richardson

The reward for family is family.

—Derrick D. Richardson

Some people make it hard for other people to do what they need to do sometimes.

—Derrick D. Richardson

When is a quote a good quote? As soon as you can see yourself in it.

—Derrick D. Richardson

You can have a relationship and career—in that order. When you change the order, you change the relationship.

—Derrick D. Richardson

A place is just a place. What happens there makes it special.

—Derrick D. Richardson

I value friendship over money. When the money is gone, a friend will still be there.

—Derrick D. Richardson

Adapting to the environment is not selling out; it's getting in where you fit in.

—Derrick D. Richardson

The truth is free. It's the lies that cost us.

—Derrick D. Richardson

Don't waste your time taking criticism from someone you can't learn from.

—Derrick D. Richardson

I don't want kids. I don't need a replica of me. I get enough of me with me.

—Derrick D. Richardson

Good friendships are hard to come by. When you have one, you cherish it. When you lose one, you never forget it.

—Derrick D. Richardson

Nothing looks good hanging unless it's meant to.

—Kathleen R. Richardson

When you finally have what you want, don't waste time wondering *why now?* Life is too short when you have one.

—Kathleen R. Richardson

Your problems are always going to be there, but you don't have to allow them to control your life. You can live life outside your problems.

—Kathleen R. Richardson

If you tell all your secrets, you won't have anything to keep to yourself.

—Donald Holiday

I'm comfortable with who I am; others, often, are not.

—S.G.

The common school is the greatest discovery made by man.

—Horace Mann

You don't need to outrun the bear; just the person with you.

—Unknown

Everybody is ignorant, only on different subjects.

—Will Rogers

The definition of insanity is doing the same thing over and over again and expecting different results.

—Albert Einstein

Twenty years from now, you'll be more disappointed by the things you didn't try than by the ones you did. So, throw off the bowlines, sail away from the safe harbor, catch the trade winds in your sails, explore, dream, and discover.

—Mark Twain

Don't take yourself so seriously that no one else has to.

—Bob Fox

How can we complain about this generation when we had everything to do with it?

—Unknown

Grandchildren are God's way of saying thanks for being a parent.

—Bill Kessler

Money doesn't cure the pain on the inside.

—Birdman

It is always easier for a parent to suffer than to watch his child in torment

—Anonymous

Nothing is impossible; we just don't know it yet.

—F. Ryan Bemis

Successful people do the things they dislike or hate in order to achieve the goals they must desire.

—Robert Whitener

You need people in your life who charge your battery, not people who will drain it.

—Robert Gentry

Knowledge is sometimes the enemy of faith.

—Unknown

If you think you can, or you think can't, you are always right.

—Henry Ford

Has the cost of living gone up or do we just want more?

—Anonymous

Tell me, and I will forget. Show me, and I will remember. Involve me, and I will understand forever.

—Confucius

An eye for an eye leaves everyone blind.

—Rev. Dr. Martin Luther King Jr.

I'll be glad when Christmas is over so people can start acting like themselves again.

—Anonymous

If a cluttered desk signs a cluttered mind, of what, then, is an empty desk a sign?

—Albert Einstein

The difficulty lies not so much in developing new ideas as in escaping from the old ones.

—John Maynard Kynes

Money just makes you more of what you already are.

—Unknown

Life affords no greater responsibility, no greater privilege, than the raising of the next generation.

—C. Everett Koop

Never doubt that a small group of thoughtful, committed citizens can change the world. Indeed, it is the only thing that ever has.

—Margaret Mead

Photos bring back memories when ours begin to fade.

—Kandice Hughes

Complaining is like sitting in a rocking chair. It gives you something to do, but doesn't get you anywhere

—Unknown

The only reward for a husband to bring home his paycheck is sex from his wife.

—Maurice White

Prayer is nothing else than being on terms of friendship with God.

—St. Teresa

Faith works in either direction.

—Unknown

They say if you want to hear God laugh, tell him your plan.

—Anonymous

When you feel like there is nowhere to turn, turn to prayer.

—Debra Pohlman

Men give women money all the time. It's just how you give it that differs.

—Anonymous

A promise between friends means you need a reason to ask why.

—Anonymous

Paradise is drifting off to sleep with someone you love.

—Anonymous

Doing what you like is freedom. Liking what you do is happiness.

—Unknown

You do not have to know where you are going to be headed in the right direction.

—Unknown

Focus on what you're doing and time will go by fast. Focus on the time and it will stand still.

—Robin Prince

In a way, hard times make you smarter—because you have to be.

—Marlissa Hudson

Music is what feelings sound like.

—Anonymous

Sometimes you have to let people feel good about doing something good for you.

—Sheila Goins

Love is what justice looks like in public.

—Unknown.

People with real style don't care about labels.

—Unknown

No one can handle your affairs better than you.

—Unknown

Being happy doesn't mean everything's perfect. It means you've decided to see beyond the imperfections.

—Unknown

Do not follow where the path may lead. Go instead where there is no path, and leave a trail.

—Anonymous

Experience is just the name we give our mistakes.

—Oscar Wilde

The fittest place for a man to die is where he dies for man.

—Elijah P. Lovejoy

A good leader will admit when he or she doesn't know the answer.

—Unknown

Great minds are always feared by lesser minds.

—Unknown

What is money worth if your mind and soul are empty?

—Unknown

All endings are also beginnings. We just don't know it at the time.

—Unknown

The moment we stop learning is the moment we give up.

—Rev. Dr. Martin Luther King Jr.

Only the guilty hold back the truth.

—Anonymous

Money and women: reasons men make the most mistakes in life.

—Anonymous

When a man and woman don't care about each other at all, they don't have a reason to fight. It's when they start out fighting all the time that there's something between them. They just don't want to admit it.

—Anonymous

The past is like an image in the rearview mirror—there to remind us of the all bad things behind us, and, most importantly, where we are now.

—Robert Whitener

People pay for what they do, and still more, for what they have become. And they pay for it simply by the lives they lead.

—Unknown

The only true currency in this bankrupt world is what you share with someone else when you're sincere.

—Unknown

There are those who create—and those who tear down.

—Unknown

Perhaps Utopia isn't an end result, but rather the simple act of striving for that result.

—Anonymous

There will always be somebody who will try to make sense out of nonsense.

—Unknown

People you try to do business with might not work with you in the beginning. Only after they see that you are successful without them will they give you the respect you deserve.

—S. Williams

Printed in the United States
By Bookmasters